Bring your D.O.G. to Work:

A (Green) Person's Best Friend-

The dog-gone easy guide to sustainability in the work place.

CHRISTINA KULL MARTENS

DEDICATION

Dedicated to my eco-lovin' friends at Virginia Tech
Who perished in the shooting in 2007.
Here's hoping I can fulfill
some of your environmental dreams for you!

CONTENTS

ACKNOWLEDGMENTS

Special thanks to my husband, Lyonel, my family,
and my book club for sticking with me
through the evolution of this book. Your helpful comments,
pitty laughs at my bad jokes, and encouragement
kept this project going!

SECTION 1
WELCOME!
PULL UP A VIRTUAL CHAIR AND LET'S CHAT.

1 LET'S HAVE SOME FUN.

C'mon boy, let's have some fun!

We've all learned that scaring people about environmental problems doesn't work to motivate them to make a change. For example: people (me) read a book on how chemicals in your beauty and cleaning products are killing them and their world. They get suddenly animated, put down the book, clean out all of their medicine cabinets and cleaning closets of anything that has any of those bad items in that book, and put them in a box. They vow to drop them off at a household hazardous waste (HHW) roundup that weekend and buy only sustainable, natural, non-toxic materials on the way home.

Ah, we've made a world of difference, right? Well, they (guilty, again, me) get to Saturday and haven't researched a HHW roundup, so it'll happen next weekend, right? Then, mid-week they have to clean up the house because the in-laws are coming over for dinner, and gosh-darn-it, the new eco-glass cleaner didn't make it into the shopping cart, so you think,

"Just this once, let's still use this bad one, and then go purchase the product that will save the world." Then, other products also start migrating back out of that box because fear, ultimately, wears off, and we return to the status quo.

So how about making work, life, and saving the world…fun? After all, if you're not having fun at work, why do you go? We have fun at home, don't we? Shouldn't we be able to make what we do every day be fun, have meaning, and make our lives, our communities, and our work environments so much better? After all, if you don't act, then you have to accept the status quo. And I'd much rather accept a workplace and relationships with my peers that is more Google©-esq (Sleeping pods! Quiddich matches!) than like a dungeon (aka, where most of us work).

2 THE D.O.G. GONE SOLUTION

You can tell they're happy if their tail is wagging.

According to a 2013 Gallup poll, 70 percent of the people in the USA are unhappy with their jobs- their status- their life. Are you one of them? In the search for meaning in all that we do, answering those questions, "What am I doing here", "What can I do to make it better?", and "Do I prefer crunchy or creamy peanut butter?" we usually throw up our hands in exasperation. Or, we get this deer in the headlights look, with our mouths agape, when we try to process visions of recycling symbols, paper coffee cups, factories and polar bears flying at us all at once and clobbering us in the forehead.

The solution? 42. Just kidding (that's the answer to the Ultimate Question of Life, the Universe, and Everything in the Hitchhikers Guide to the Galaxy (Yup, I'm an eco-dork.))

Rather, the solution is Doing. Our. Greenest. (D.O.G. if you want an acronym). I'm not talking about taking a vow to recycle your bank statements and call it a year (truly, you should opt for their e-notices, at least to avoid the paper cuts); I'm saying you could build on what you do that adds value and makes you happy in your personal life and see it translate into your professional life. That's kinda like being able to bring your dog to work!

Workplace translation: it's like setting up a white paper recycling box (made from the box the paper came in) beside your huge printer-copier-faxer combo in the office with a kitschy PowerPoint©-made sign on it that states:

"Help us turn PAPER into WINE.
White Paper Recycling Here-
Profits go to the Employee Wine-Tasting Club."

Look at that! You just solved a problem that everyone else in the office has been complaining about for years, and your wine club can now sponsor a much-needed free drink after work. You think, "Why didn't anyone else think of that?" (It's because of the Liability Insurance-- just kidding!) Your peers are thinking the same thing about you- "Why didn't any of us stand up and say, 'If not me, who will?'"...

It's because we usually think it is someone else's job- won't the Environmental Department get mad if we do this? (Wait, do we have an Environmental Department?) The reality is that many of these things fall through the cracks in workplaces (the bigger the company, the bigger and more numerous the cracks), and go-getter employees like you (you're reading this book, aren't you?) are the last chance of man-kind. Ok, the last chance of mankind might be He-Man/She-Ra or Captain Planet, but you don't have to wear funky capes or ride tigers (many are endangered after all!) to make it happen.

3 FOLLOW ME, GREEN YOU

Leading the pack...

To get your brain started, this book is a compilation of what we've done at my various workplaces. Most workplaces function like a small city- there are facilities, food, janitorial, power, water, personal space, human issues, politics, air quality concerns, waste, etc.... all problems like a real metropolis! "We" means myself and my other, let us call them, ECO-CHIC (say it like you're French- it has much more Oh-la-la exclusivity that way) coworkers at work.

What was our budget? Zero. Zilch. Nada. Niet. Can you do it? Of course! And your bosses will notice. You just solved paper recycling and employee morale in one fell swoop with that paper recycling = wine-tasting, didn't you? You're VP material! Not only your bosses, but your coworkers will applaud you... and hopefully start leaving gifts of homage on your desk You can develop a more fulfilling life in all aspects at work and home if we are just Doing. Our. Greenest.

You're probably thinking, "I need this extra thing like I need a hole in my head." Well, actually, we do need holes in our heads! What are your eyes, mouth, nostrils, ears, if not openings to let things in and out? (Yes, yucky, but they are necessary.) Humans tend to reject or bristle against change. Ergo, BEING that instrument of change can thus be perceived to be VERY HARD.

The only way you can eat an endangered elephant is 1 bite at a time. To get started, I suggest you STOP looking at the big picture; because sometimes you just need small Polaroid's of action (those are like hard copy Instagram's, for my Millennials). It won't be complete in one lunch break, but it can be done in a lifetime of little moments of Doing. Our. Greenest.

So take a moment to decide to bring your D.O.G. to your workplace, and in the process have more fun yourself. To rip off Ghandi, start "Be(ing) the change you wish to see in the world" workplace!

SECTION 2
SOME OF MY FAVORITE THINGS

4 FOOD

Puppy Chow.

Let's talk about my favorite subject- food! (Thought I was going to say sustainability, didn't you?) This subject, other than, maybe, "Did that guy my sister went out with last night have a tongue piercing?" is probably the most common thing on your mind throughout today. Food is a central facet of our lives both in and out of the bubbles we call our office, car and home.

Here are some ways to get you started Doing. Our. Greenest., in a tasty fashion on some simple projects. They are all fashioned after a complaint or hurdle we've actually come across in our workplaces, and can show you some of the simple (and usually free) ways we've found around it. Here's how to do it from starting up, to keeping up, one paw print at a time. Let's chow down, lil' doggies!

"My bosses don't provide me with reusable plates and mugs **in the break area.**"

Did your realtor provide you a set of China when you moved into your first apartment? No! Just like college, you usually get something used that someone no longer wants because they've moved onto something different.

• We all know that person in the office that has *yikes*, unsustainable purchasing habits. Say, she's just upgraded to the latest china set from the department store, so why not have her old set in the work cupboards? Remember your kitschy PowerPoint© sign for the "Turn paper into wine" equation? Do a sign here requesting an old dish set donation taped above your coffee pot.

• One of our teams annual fundraisers for our company's prime charity is a Reuse Rummage Sale. We get at least 3 sets of dishes a year. They don't always sell because they are incomplete (missing those little dishes for under the tea cups, I bet!). The team washes them and puts them into the cupboards at one of my green members break room/kitchen areas. We also include a sign that says "Your mother doesn't work here-if you use it, wash it".... or something nicer if you work in the Human Resources department.

"The cafeteria forces me to use a disposable tray!"

Arrrggh, the agony of having too much great food at your onsite cafeteria (not a common issue for people)! This usually means trays. In workplaces that are trying to get you to go back to your desk and work through your lunch break, this means disposable trays, as the cafeteria doesn't think you're ever coming back after you taste today's mystery meat special.

• A solution? Reusable trays, just like the ever popular reusable cups. Worried about them not coming back? Let the employees "own" them, and even put their name on them (we had a leaf shape imprinted where employees put their name and phone number in case they misplaced it).

• But how do you pay for that? Simple. What was the cost of the disposable trays? Have your café manager pay it forward and use that to purchase reusables-these trays paid for themselves (at ~$1/each) within 8 months, and then the rest is pure profit for them. Now that's some dough we can enjoy!

"Those cafeteria stuff is cluttering up my trashcan!"

Congratulations! You made it all the way through that mystery meat special, but now have the trappings of a quick and queasy meal left over. Taking a note from our disposable tray dilemma, do we need to purchase all reusables for our employees? You could, but an easier and free route that we offered here was discounts for using reusables employees already owned in our cafeterias.

• Bring your own coffee mug? We'll take the price of the physical coffee cup (and extra hot sleeve and lid- total $0.06) out of the price you pay for your morning Coffee.

• Bring your own ToGo Ware© utensils and/or People Towel ©? Then we're takin' off $0.10 in costs.

• Now the big one- decide to dine in the cafeteria, reclaim your lunch break while using a reusable plate? We're taking off between $0.14 and $0.28!

Woohoo- you just saved yourself enough to buy one of those TicTac boxes at the checkout (what WERE you thinking with the mystery meat selection, after all?). And now your office trash can will thank you.

"Employees never use those eco-giveaways!"

Remember: Pledges hold power

Whenever you give something away (say, for Earth Day or a cafeteria greening project like the reusable trays), you should have the recipient's sign a pledge that they will USE it. Excel-made forms are an easy solution, but when taped up on the Cafeteria wall after pledging, they have little visual appeal. How about instead showing the item they are pledging to use? Jackpot! Wall art.

• For the Earth Day 25th anniversary we gave away reusable bags and trees (yay!-free from the Forest service). My "Goth" high school intern (they get class credit working with us) was doodling when I returned one day to our cubicle (yes- we always shared a humble cubicle). The doodles were AMAZING!

• So, I asked if he had any interest in drawing our Earth Day poster, the kid lit up like a non-forest-fire-starting firecracker. I showed him the giveaways, and he took the project home to work on it.

• I'll repeat that, because you probably just missed it. HE TOOK THE PROJECT HOME TO WORK ON IT! (unusual for teenagers). Resulting poster made from backs of old ethics posters: a smiling grizzly bear holding our company reusable bag in front of a tree, stating "Celebrate Earth Day, Every day".

• We had everyone who took a green giveaway sign their names to the pledge poster, then displayed the posters in the cafeteria as a reminder. These pledge posters lasted an ENTIRE YEAR displayed in our cafeterias, until our next Earth Day poster (and a new intern masterpiece) was rolled out.

"We don't have a cafeteria, so we have to go out for fast food!"

Have you ever noticed how fast food is not that fast? You've got to lock your computer (so coworkers don't send joke emails from your account), find your wallet and keys, walk out, get in your super eco-car, drive to the strip mall, wait in the drive through, remind the cashier you wanted no salt- No Salt!, pay, drive back to your office, park, walk inside, dodge your peers when they smell the French Fries, avoid being way-laid by your boss about the TPS report covers (ok- enough Office Space© references), and finally spread out your food and gulp it down before your 1 hr break is up. *Sigh!*

• In contrast, I just timed it- my baked potato (on one of those handy reusable plates we stocked our break room with) just took under 10 minutes to cook in the break room microwave with a cheddar/broccoli/ham mix. Yummmmmm.

• Let's see, that means I have about 50 more minutes to write this book for you in my lunch hour! Woohoo! Just think... even those all in one microwavable meals take under10 minutes and create less waste (both in personal car emissions, trash, and caloric by-product) than those "fast" foods you scurried out for.

• Don't get me wrong- there IS big value in going out with your coworkers for engagement and team building- I put a "lunch out of the office" on my calendar at least one time a week. We go out and discuss weekend plans, the meaning of the universe, and things like, "Did you see what the boss wore today?" with my peers.

What could you do with that extra 50 minutes in your day?

5 THE CUBE

Breaking out of the Pound.

I've heard many people liken an office cubicle to a prison cell. Think about it- it's approximately the same size, you've got a roommate that you didn't choose, you feel locked into it for 8 hours a day, and you frequently take meals and do mundane daily tasks in it (ever waited for a phone customer service rep from your bank? Just like prison.). Viewed this way, it IS a prison... But what about us Doing. Our. Greenest. at work and having fun while doing it?

As a geekily trained scientist and engineer (albeit one that has a oddball sense of humor and can actually speak to other humans), I prefer to see the cubicle as a petri dish...you can do all sorts of experiments in there! (Preferable not on your cube-mate, but in your own section of that 6'x6' box).

Quick, before your cube-mate barks at you, let's get some experiments going in this puppy!

"My office trash can smells and doesn't get picked up enough!"

Wow- that WOULD smell like a science experiment! It's just like at home- I HATE that my midnight snack stays in my bedside trashcan for weeks before it's picked up by my live-in butler.

Wait, you don't have a bedside trashcan? Or a butler? What about the obligatory hanging-off-the-back-of-the-living-room-couch-trash bin? You don't have those EITHER? Where do you live...America? So why do you have an office trash can? Aren't we all worried about gaining weight by too sedentary a job?

• One of the things our ECO-CHIC volunteers choose to do is to get rid of their trash cans or flip them over so it looks more like a foot stool. We don't need the individual trash cans!!!

So follow us and can (pun intended) the individual trash bin habit, and make mini-trips to a centralized bin in the break room to eliminate your guilty evidence of a 2 PM sugar binge.

"I need lots of electronics in my cubicle to be efficient."

I have this picture of one of the tiniest and nerdiest cubicles I've ever seen, jam-packed with electronics...

• Here's their list: 2 monitors, a CPU, a laptop, a docking station, speakers, under cabinet light, Radio/CD player, mini fridge, microwave, coffee pot, bottled water distributor, plant grow light (dead plant underneath), printer/scanner/fax, desktop fan, floor heater, chair heater/massager, cell phone charger, iPod charger and docking station, electric pencil sharpener, electric stapler, electric 3-hole punch, a phone and a meditation water fountain (a little too close to one overloaded circuit for my comfort).

• And guess what? They were ALL turned on after hours before a loooooong holiday weekend. The kicker? Their cubicle was immediately beside one of our kitchenettes and a managed printing center on the other. Seem redundant? (say yes)

• So, during these audits we have little papers that use green slogans like, "The Chairs don't need to see- please turn off your desk lamp!" that we leave in energy-sucking cubicles. This cubicle needed SO MANY that I ended up just taking a piece from the adjacent paper recycling bin, and wrote "CALL ME – I CAN HELP!: x5419" and taped it to their monitor. Then killed the power to their little glowing city.

• After this experience the employee ended up with a laptop, light, 2 monitors and a docking station with USB ports to charge/run items from the USB port in their computer (that stop pulling power when your computer shuts down). Oh, and we let them keep their chair massager, because we're not masochists.

"It's too bright in my office/cube!"

Arrrgggh, the horror of first world countries and of not being able to slip into a nap because of all those bright lights in your air conditioned office! ⬜ Ok, seriously my work area now contains one of the coolest lighting motion sensors I've ever seen. It controls 2 sets of fluorescent lights in fixtures.

So why am I being difficult? The second fixture doesn't light ANY of my work space- and I'm sure that fake plant in that corner doesn't care if it gets any light.

• My solution? I put a small sticky note over the 2nd sensor. Now that light doesn't come on anymore. That's a daily savings of a whopping $0.19 a day (130 watts/fixture x 10 hrs x $0.145/kWh). However, based on the days I work per year, that comes out to about $42 annually. That's the best return on investment for a single sticky note I've ever seen!

• No motion sensor? Off switches with a sticky note above saying "Saving energy-don't turn on!" or taping switches in the off positon works wonders, too.

6 DECORATING THE DOG HOUSE

A dog's house is his kingdom

Are you surrounded by 4 cloth walls in a prison-like setting that has seen better days? Do you cringe when you walk by impersonal spaces that look so sterile and depressing that a robot must work there? Broke? Well, you're in luck- here are several ways to personalize your personal space, and make a statement about your green convictions at work. It's a better way to mark your territory than other ways D.O.G.'s do...

1- Plant it.

• No, I don't mean go splurge on an orchid (those \$%^& things die quickly even though you SWEAR you have a green thumb). I'm talking about a pull out of the ground; get as a clipping from a friend; or a start-a-tomato-seed-from-your-lunch-in-your-coffee-grounds-from-breakfast kind of plant. Even a single sprig of Rosemary you nipped off the plant when you walked into the office from the parking lot will do in a pinch (just don't tell the landscaper!).

• Most plants can garner the light they need from fluorescent office lights (they release a wide band), the plants cheer you up, and they actually clean your air Me, I've got a spider plant in an empty coffee can planted in worm casings from my home bin (that's worm poop for your lay people) and some mulch bark left over from that orchid I killed (opps, did I just admit that was me?)."Spidey" (I name my cars, too) looks great, and is phenomenal in removing Formaldehyde from the air (that's the "New office smell" off-gassing from your furniture...).

It sure kicks the fronds off of that plastic palm tree in the corner of my office (Hopefully the real plant is absorbing the fake plant fumes? How cool is that?)

2-   Rip it

• Pinned against my wall in my office is a postcard from a tree-lovin' non-profit org. that I tore from a magazine in college. John Muir's quote, "Going to the woods, is going home" is overlaid on a picture of a sheer cliff with a waterfall and a forest encircling it all. It's the first thing I put up when I move into a new location, and is always where I can stare at it while looking like I'm doing work ("My boss just yelled at me. Why do I do this work again? Oh, yeah, to save the world.").

• You can find similar things in all of your favorite eco-magazines, websites or even that eco-non-profit that won't stop sending you those address stickers after you sent them $15 back in college). Heck, you could even decorate with those address labels! They usually have endangered animals or baby tigers on them. (My recycling bin at home is covered in 'em.)

3-   Pin It

• Every one of us thinks we are marketing geniuses. When starting our green teams, management wanted to kick off the program with a splashy start (sound familiar, like every company that has ever existed?), and decided we would do a slogan and poster competition. We used some of the slogans on small signs in the conference rooms above the light switches (Ex: "Earth! Wind! Fire! …The Power is Yours! ©Turn off the Light & Projector"…yes, one employee did channel Captain Planet©), and used others on banners and our new website.

• Then, management got too excited and printed too many posters and banners, so we gave away extras to departments and employees who wanted to hang them from their hallways.

• All of the old posters from our events also got a turn decorating my cubicle walls. One year, we covered the entire length of the hallway with a "History of the green team" display, pinning up all our old posters from our beginning to the current Earth Day Festival. It was the most colorful April Earth-month, EVER, in our department!

4- Recycle it

• I'm not joking! Make them CLEAN recyclables, though, otherwise you'll get visits from creepy-crawly friends. It all started with our cafeteria greening project. We compiled all the materials that were currently recycled, recyclable, recycled content, etc and I needed to create a visual encompassing it. The floor didn't work for picture contrast, but one of my cubicle walls was a nice, empty blue. I busted out some thumbtacks and up the recyclables went!

• Whenever someone came over and said, "Well, what's new in green?" I could physically show them what the eco-team was working on. So it was a free, changing display depending on the project, and actually looked like contemporary art

5-   Draw it

• Just like in college, I have a dry erase board where I work. I diagram projects on it, I draw on it, my peers write me messages, and we stick cool examples of thought ware on it with magnets. This area keeps people busy when they walk into my office and I'm on the phone and give them the "1 minute!" hand gesture (not THAT finger- get your mind out of the gutter!).

• Long running crossword puzzles have emerged on it, I've reconstructed entire Family Day event concepts there, and can use it as my way of showing the boss what I'm working on (so I can then ask them WHICH item I should get rid of when they bring a new project to me...Strangely, bosses always just write the   new   task   at   the   bottom   of   the   list...)

SECTION 3
SIZE IT UP

7 SWEAT THE SMALL STUFF

Puppies grow into their paws...

Let's go small- like fits onto your desktop kind of small- for things you can do at work. Doing. Our. Greenest. doesn't have to be installing solar panels at work- it can be doing things around us to realize a greener setting and new normal. It's all about the little steps...after all- little puppies grow into their huge paw prints!

"I don't want to walk to the recycling bin every time I throw a piece of paper away…"

(Hmm, why don't we ever say "every time I *recycle* a piece of paper?" There is no "Away")

• We all want to do free wine tasting from paper recycling profits, so we solved employee laziness with desktop recyclers. Started with the copier paper box lids and with hand written "Recycle paper here" messages. Well, as we were hoping, management didn't want something so crass looking all over their facility (hey! It was free and you told me there was no budget for recycling), so they ponied up $300 for us to get materials for desktop recyclers.

• Yay! Until we realized we needed to cover 4,000 employees. One employee suggested foldable cardboard boxes at $0.12 each. With two people in every cube, we only needed 2,000 of them at one box per cube. BINGO! Budget saved.

• We printed nice looking printed labels for them (from Surplus Office Supplies! More on those later) and made it a competition for 2 competing "manufacturing lines" to assemble them, and used that last $40 to buy pizza for the 2 teams.

• Next, we simply left a HUGE box of them at the entrance with a sign "Please put one at your cube. Empty into centralized paper recycling bins when full!" The huge box was empty by week end!

• Our facilities guys now buy, fold and distribute them so they save themselves time and money by not throwing away the bins when they clean out an area- (that was the best delegation we've ever done for keeping a recycling program running!).

"What is that? A Two-Can Toucan?"

Come dork out with me for a minute.

• Recycled cans/bottles can be used for Cangineering Design Challenges. What is that? Well, if you work in an engineering company, like I have, then you may have heard of National Engineers Week. We get together and drop eggs from 2 stories up, build towers out of pasta and marshmallows (I eat a lot of marshmallows in the process), students come and shadow engineers, and employees build art out of cans (thus, can(en)gineering.)

• One year, the teams were told the company could no longer pay to buy the cans for the competition (that would afterwards get boxed and donated to our local food bank after the judging round). Our Eco-Chic club took on the challenge. We publicized a competition for turning empty, used recyclable bottles and cans into works of art. First year? Animal themed (thus the Two-can Toucan). Second year? They made our company products! And so on.

• And there WERE prizes! Competitors liked that the VP gave them a certificate and took a picture with them in a short ceremony. Most of them had never hob-knobbed with a VP before this event!

"Why don't you just go 'Click'?"

• Earth Hour can be fun- especially if you ever need an excuse for a candlelight dinner with your significant other or to be able to tell your boss you can't work! Well, www.EarthHour.org can help you out. The event, held for one hour on the last Saturday in March, just wants you to turn it all off! (for the planet)

• We've swept our buildings a day in advance of Earth Hour to turn off excess electricity and left those little reminder notes to employees to go "CLICK". Then, our Facilities team jumped in and shut off the signage for the company and the landscaping lights.

• We take a before and after picture, and voila! It's an instant article for the local newspaper and the beginning of an eco-challenge from your company (or home) to the surrounding competitors for next year. Game on!

8 BIGGER THAN YOURSELF

(A sign over the dog's dish) "Recycle Bones Here"

Some ways of Doing.Our.Greenest. take time to implement at our homes and offices. Up to now, most of these things have been items you can tackle by yourself with no sweat off your eco-lovin' brow. But, if we want to be that change (thanks, Ghandi!), we may need to create venues for others to join us in our efforts, too. Remember, if you don't tell/show others what you're trying to accomplish, they can't join in!

"Isn't it an earth-killer to have an earth fair?"

Who would ever want to market to you and the scrubs you work with? Oh wait, everyone does- that's the entire concept for non-profits and for-profits alike!

• Get an email list of favorite local green products and organizations from your green team.

• Then, invite/evite them and let them promote green products and events to your employees.

• Make sure you tell them you're trying to go zero-waste so they don't leave you with piles of trash/recyclables to deal with.

• Heck- some of your employee teams or departments will want a booth as well! (Ex: the facilities team wants YOU to recycle...now take this desktop paper recycler with you back to your desk).

• You don't even need to buy tents or tables or chairs for a fair. Have your event in a location where you already have tables, like a cafeteria or a conference room.

• Promotion: Include words like FREE, and GIVEAWAYS, and DURING LUNCH in your emails and PowerPoint flyers (on backs of used paper). Keep it short and sweet for maximum retention.

"Why not just take the shirt off my back, why don't you…"

Ok, well, maybe the shirt in the back of my closet that doesn't fit me anymore. Just ask yourself- what causes or charities does my company already align with?

• For us, anything that supports service men and women is usually good. We gave the USO© things like extra bottled and canned drinks from large events, books/magazines for while soldiers are travelling, and repainted their facility with left over architectural paint. Here's some other ideas:

• Does your business work with or like animals? How about collecting old blankets/towels or tennis balls from your recreational clubs for animal shelters or mismatched socks for bat research? (trust me- it's a real cause)

• A group that focuses on the homeless? Collect Hotel toiletries, eye glasses (Give the Gift of Site©), gently used coats and outfits for Working Wardrobes©, and shoes for Soles for Souls© from your employees.

• Like to support kids? We send greeting card fronts to St. Jude's Ranch©, crayon stubs to be made into new kid-friendly products, and surplus office supplies to our local schools.

• All you need are paper boxes, publicity (hello, email and PowerPoint©!) and a packer (aka, someone on a lot of teleconferences). Next, we usually choose groups that have drop off locations, ones that will pick up or that will pay for shipping.

You know what your group rallies around- now go chase it, like a dog chases its tail!

SECTION 4
KEEPIN' IT IN "SITE"

9 OFFICE SUPPLIES

Who stole my bone?

Ever utter the words, "Where'd my stapler go?" after your well-deserved vacation and break from the daily grind? Office supplies tend to be hot commodities at home and, well, at offices. There never seems to be enough, and people pilfer prodigiously (say THAT 10 times fast!). Even old D.O.G.s can learn some new tricks in providing for themselves, their departments, and communities!

"What's our new company name?"

Ever come in on Monday and your division has renamed itself in the name of progress? Groan. Double groan if they didn't think through the acronym it would create! (Been there) Now, change your voicemail, email tag line, and the printed stuff. What do you do with printed stuff- you spent major money on these! Other than the Captain Obvious easy answer (recycle them), we like to get more creative. Try these:

• Old Business cards? Make them "while you were out" messages- flipped over to the blank back with your message- and no need to write your name or how to contact me- it's on the back!

• Thank You Cards? A paper cutter takes off that old name and logo along the bottom and now makes our holiday cards.

• Printed letter head? Cut in quarters, flipped and stapled they become scratch note pads. (We admittedly turned a few into paper airplanes that we tried to land in the recycle bin).

• Envelopes? Print new address labels and stuck 'em over the old return address.

The pièce de résistance? If we had any future items pre-printed we try to avoid putting any tag lines or division names on them, and made electronic templates that printed the logo and letterhead at the same time at the top of the letter (so no pre-printed stacks of paper). This caused less demand to reprint items when my division was renamed in the future, saves me some waste (but it did eliminate some excuses to hold a paper airplane contest).

"They are moving my cubicle. Again."

"Thus, I'll just throw this away- no one would EVER need this 3-hole punch." Later your kid says, "I broke a 3-hole punch. You need to buy my class a new one." Don't you wish you get your unwanted work 3-hole punch to the school?

• Let's bridge the gap- first, find out who's in charge of office supplies, and say "We want to:

o **Step 1. Collect what people throw away,**
o **Step 2. Offer it back to employees,**
o **Step 3. Then give extras to schools,**
o **Step 4. AND save the company THOUSAND$."**

• Now-you've just saved work money for waste hauling costs and new equipment purchases, got a hefty tax write-off for what they gave to the school, and become parent of the year.

• How do you pull it off? Our Admins print a premade flyer, staple it to an empty box, and send an email to their team that XYZ location is a drop off so we can donate the extra to schools. Tell them they can also utilize supplies from this area.

• What schools to pick? Let your green volunteers nominate them, then just check them off based on first nominated and is within lunchtime driving distance. Or invite the schools over, put all the stuff in a conference room, and let the schools pick what they need.

Your employees will thank you, too- seriously, who has never raided a co-workers cubicle the hour after their retirement party? I know you've coveted that phone headset of Mindy's for years, and she's driving off into the sunset to no more conference calls...

"Is this FOR ORF?"

Nope, not a misspelling or a strange form of dyslexia, it's one of those crazy cleanup strategies our green team has. Originally meaning "Operation Round File" (ORF) (the "Round File" was the trash can), the green team has co-opted this practice and the acronym to become "Operation Recycle File".

• Stay with me now. Before employees move, a trio of functions (Facilities, Recordkeeping, and our green team) led the effort to get employees to sort through their office spaces, supplies, and records to clean up their act- literally, in as little as a week's time.

• Emails go out, flyers go up, supply boxes are placed, paper recycling bins line the hallways, our shredder company commits to recycle the paper, and training is offered for recordkeeping. Win/win for saving money, space, resources, staying in compliance and saving the world, all in a day's work

10 SITE CELEBRATIONS

Have your kibble and eat it too.

Are celebrations and work always mutually exclusive of one another? I bet your kibble that they are not! From Earth Days, to Work Family Picnics, to Milestone Celebrations, companies strive to recognize and engage their employees by celebrating those cornerstones that make the organizations and their employee populations, tick. Here's how to keep the D.O.G. from outgrowing its kennel with the eco-impacts of such celebrations.

"They say the easiest way to go is disposables."

When you hold site celebrations, they can be A LOT OF WORK. On one side of the scale is doing a small booth for earth day in your cafeteria. You need volunteers, giveaways or activities, messaging, and prep and event time away from your regular job (and that's just for 1 cafeteria table for 2 hrs on Earth Day that will hit around 100 people).

• Now, imagine doing that for a 10,000 person Family Day at your location! It can get overwhelming if you don't eat that endangered elephant one bite at a time. In the mix of making sure that you remember tell catering to place the ice with the drinks, finding where facilities stored the time capsule you're supposed to unveil, and keeping to your budget, many of the actions you can take to minimize your ecological footprint during the event run right out the door (pun intended)!

• To counteract that, we always put a person on our team whose sole focus is "sustainability". That used to be me on teams, but as you go up in your green career, you'll need others to be that person- even for you! Sure, they will point out when you have a spelling mistake in the flyer, but their main focus is to let us know when we are missing an eco-opportunity.

Here are some eco-opportunities that our team had from a recent event:

• Having hamburgers at your event? Consider also a veggie burger option.

• Can you use large reusable pumps and containers for the mustard and ketchup?

• Can you serve meals in a compostable paper boat instead of Styrofoam or metal wrap? Then just have compost bins to collect waste that day.

• Having to use bottled water? Place recycling bins with signage everywhere people pick up bottles or throw away trash to close the loop.

• Had to use a bus last time to shuttle visitors from 1 area to another? Try decreasing the footprint on your event so it's walkable.

• Spent too much money on a rented tent and disposable warming trays to feed people? Use your existing cafeteria to hand out the food.

• Threw away all your welcome signs, directional signs, maps, etc from last time because you put the year and date on them? Let's make them generic so you can reuse them again next time.

• Couldn't GIVE away the extra goodies later from the event as prizes at your company because they said Family Day on it? Why not just put your company logo on it instead.

• And the opportunities continue...

11 THE HOLIDAYS

After the Dog-Days of summer...

When the dog-days of summer are done, and we're getting into the months of Holidays, Doing. Our. Greenest. can get challenging. We like to give and to get, and the thing that gets the short end of the stick is usually sustainability. Instead of sticks (even if we're D.O.G.s), try using some of these carrots! (then the Reindeer will love you)

"Do they like me, or are they trying to get more business?"

I get tons of holiday cards at work and home... Coworkers being nice. Contractors trying to remind me they should be hired again. Once a year Family communications. Friends who live far away. Cards from people we don't know that don't realize their friends don't live at our address anymore. After the glow of the Holiday season, what do you do with the cards? Well, I tear mine up... but in a nice way.

• I cut off the backs and recycle them. The fronts I save and add to the Birthday and thank you card fronts from the rest of the year, and bring them into a bin at work we set up every January in the lobby (we promote that it will be there in December to get employees primed to act sustainably).

• We gather the card fronts, box 'em, and send them to St. Jude's Ranch for Children for their Card Recycling Program. St. Jude's then sorts them, glues new backs on them, then sells them in bunches as a fundraiser for their charity.

I'm hoping one day to get one of my cards back in its new form, from a charitable eco-minded friend... or maybe from those Contractors who are trying to stand out!

(To the tune of The 12 Days of Christmas©...)

"On the first day of Christmas, my true love gave to me...
... a Dead Tre-e in the Lobb-y"

Wow, that would not catch on as a Christmas Jingle, so why do we do it at our businesses? We stopped killing trees for "joy" my second year at one company. Here's how:

• We met a cool company that rents potted, living, holiday trees. We asked if they wanted to market for free to my employees so that they might be influenced to decorate more sustainably. They said yes, and loaned us a tree FOR FREE to use in decorating our highest trafficked lobby.

• The green team decorated the tree with a sign about the company and with second hand decorations and LED-lights. The company's rentals went up, employees got a discount, and our company didn't have to pay to kill a tree or buy decorations that year. Winning!!!

• Each year we recruited more employee teams to adopt a living lobby tree. The teams decorated it, watered it, and then took the decorations down before vacation. Though slightly costlier than the murdered tree, we could run the program cheaper than before. Now, employee teams from our PriDA (stunning rainbow colored decorations) to the Asian Pacific Islanders group (Tahitian head dress and grass skirt on their tree) get to show off to employees and garner more members.

• Oh- and there is ALWAYS a green team tree- we parceled out Parsley seed packets (say that 10 times fast) recently, my Santa Hat as the crowning glory, and free LED lights from exchanging old donated incandescent lights in with the electric utility. Now THAT's a green tree!

"Remember-Don't get trashed at the holiday party!"

If your company is lucky enough to have a holiday party (yeah, you might groan about it, but wait until you are at a company that doesn't host anything!), you'll notice it is a bastion of waste. For us, it's potluck style with a white elephant gift exchange, as we still want to celebrate with our co-workers and friends (and frenemies, too, I guess).

• It usually goes like this- people bring in too many deserts, everyone's on a diet, and people don't want to bring their food back home. So, many of us looked for full circle solutions to this annual carnage. I now claim beverages- two 3-liters of different drinks (since we recycle the bottles and compost the cups) or pitchers of lemonade or tea (sorry, not spiked-it's at work-I'm not talking about THAT kind of "trashed!").Thus, there are never any leftovers for me to worry about.

• Others have started to bring in reusable take home containers as their contribution (when no easy way exists to bring things home, events always end with items going in the trash).

• Another brings everyone potato starch cutlery to use that can be composted.

• Another person brings his own plate, glass, to-go ware, and reusable napkin and then brings home a bag of compostables to his cities green waste bin.

• Then on to the gift giving. The most popular gift would be... bottles of alcohol, but that's banned at our company. So, the legal gift that's best is...gift cards! Sure- it may take the funny out of seeing someone open a Snuggy ©, but it can significantly reduce your packaging and re-gifting.

SECTION 5
GET OUT!

12 THE GREAT OUTDOORS

Remember to wipe your paws.

What kind of environmentalist would I be if I didn't have anything about the outdoors in my book? Well, I'd still be an excellent environmentalist! (There's not a chapter only dedicated to only recycling, either!) We spend most of our lives indoors, so we shouldn't be ashamed of making the great INDOORS as green as the great OUTDOORS.

If you're like me, though, at some point you have to at least walk from your apartment to your car to your office (unless you live in snow-covered parts of Canada, and then I totally understand your underground parking and walkways!) Guess what? You could even bring your D.O.G. with you!

"Book Nerds Rule"-(not what you expected to kick off a chapter about the outdoors, huh?)

That's right- a lot of our employees are nerds and like books. They read 'em then they donate 'em.

• Work has spawned several book clubs, though we may not necessarily meet at work (you can't drink wine there). I host at my house, and the host gets to pick the book that's read (we are at the whims of whoever holds the monthly crown). So, since I've plodded through instructional books on fishing, romance novels, and teen-heartthrob best sellers from other hosts, you can guess what my topics have been on! It was Food and Wood Chucking Wood-Chucks (not a real book). Just kidding- topics have been on sustainability (at this time I reserve the "write" to choose the Wood chucking wood-chucks topic if ever a book shall cross my path).

• The first year, I was really working on how to up the ante in marketing for my green teams, so we read What Women Want (no, not the movie). It's a book on marketing, which helped tremendously with how we do eco-booths at fairs for Earth Day and Eco-Week (Did you know if it's too neat, no one will take an eco-pledge giveaway from your display?).

• The next year, a gift from my older sister was highlighted- Zero Impact Man (and there's a movie, so we watched that as part of the book club since I know some of my members don't always read, err, finish, the books).

• This year, I was trying to inspire many of my members to do sustainable gardens. All the food at the event was vegetarian, spiced with the herbs from my tiny 4'x12' backyard garden, and demonstrated many of the eco-gardening processes I use while we sat in my own garden.

"They just threw away the new-ish plants from outside the front lobby!"

Here's my "Free Friday Floral Frenzy" shout out to the City of Alexandria, VA- they are where we heard this idea! Several times a year, business parks will pay someone to tear out their old annuals, and pay them to plant new annuals three to four times a year!

• Instead, let's allow the employees to take the flowers and bring them home to their own gardens! We publicize it, tell people to bring their shovels & boxes and let them take all the flowers they want. Voila! You've just saved half the cost of your landscaping labor.

• Also, consider letting the Boy/Girl Scout-type troops come in, too (maybe hold the event on a weekend if you invite them)- then they can take the flowers as part of their service projects for replanting at schools, churches, retirement homes, etc. I bet they'd even sweep up the dirt for you as a thank you...

"Why don't you just take a hike?"

(Now this is more like what you expected for the outdoors chapter, yeah?)

No, don't quit your job- a hike is simply a walk outdoors (that was fun to explain to my French-speaking Sister-in-law the first time we met).

• Our eco-team formed a partnership with the healthy living groups at work for lunch time walks. We even made maps of routes at 1 mile, 2 miles, etc.

• We walk, talk, ogle neighboring business complexes shameful use of water to grow inappropriate-but-gorgeous-flowers here in the desert, and get to know our fellow employees better with some fresh air (though clean air is sometimes debatable in Los Angeles with smog).

13 COMMUNITY EVENTS

Friends Fur-ever.

How close do you live to where you work? If you're an average American, it can be about <u>50 miles</u> round trip between home-sweet-home and your paycheck giver. Why? Is where you work not really "nice"? Does it have a weak community feel? Are the parks and social spaces not up to snuff? What can we do about that?

If you work someplace that you couldn't see yourself walking your real dog, then there's opportunity for community involvement and partnerships. Just because you work in an industrial area doesn't mean it should be a place devoid of vegetation and trees, with littered beaches and parks, and run-down community centers or walking trails.

Use some of these ways to partner with your local communities to help create a network of sustainability, and you'll see the partnerships will guarantee Friends Fur-ever.

"Who works for others on the weekend?"

Well, I do! I work for my community, my church, my friends, my family, etc...work is just how you define it. Our company "gets our green on" volunteering for other groups that usually have the materials, but just need the elbow grease or rippling muscles available from a bunch of desk-bound office workers.

• We've planted flowers at inner-city schools, yanked out invasive weeds near the baseball stadium, mulched a teaching garden at a middle school, painted low VOC murals in parks, and tilled soil and pruned fruit trees for the Veterans Affairs Hospital Garden.

Seeing my coworkers in this light (and sometimes with dirt smudged on their noses) with their families and friends in tow definitely makes for much more interesting conversation around the coffee pot on Mondays.

"What's a corporation doing at the City Earth Day fair?"

Who would ever want to hear what we're doing for sustainability through our company? Oh, wait, that's everybody- employees, community members, and elected officials all are hungry for information.

• Want us for your Cities Wellness fair? We'll set up a "collect your old shoes booth" for Soles for Souls ©, and answer questions about what else our green team does. Cost for booth? $0! We're doing a service, and getting to promote our green successes at the same time.

• Have a Community Center Earth Day event? We'll set up our green trivia wheel. Tiny kids love to spin it (and adults love it, too, if you pretend they are on Wheel of Fortune) and answer a green trivia question (and at least learn something), and we give them free cool stuff we've found from our surplus office supply cleanouts (eg: outdate t-shirts, lanyards, luggage tags, etc).

• Having a community carbon reduction celebration and need a parking lot for participants to park in and catch a bus pool over to the event? We're your guys! Great news? You're then in the news for something great!

"We can't do a tree planting- it's freakin' expensive!"

Trees do actually grow on (ok, from,) trees, but can be expensive to purchase. I have this great picture of a past president of my company stomping on a tree- literally! Was he frustrated at the cost of doing this eco-event? No. Actually, he was trying to loosen the root ball so he could get it out of its pot to plant it, but it's my favorite blackmail picture of him.

• Trees, if you try to go down and just buy them big at a home improvement store are expensive, so where did we get our trees? The local Air Quality District gave them to us as part of a clean air grant. Another year, the Forest Service gave some to us. Have you ever requested a seedling from the National Arbor Day Foundation©? They'll give 'em to you, too. I think I've also gotten 4 fruit trees from the Social Justice Learning Institute© in Los Angeles in as many years.

• If you're thinking, "they'll only give me a small amount for free at one time," you may be right. But remember they will give EACH MEMBER of your ECO-CHIC team a tree or two. Before you know it, you have enough for your entire company to gather round and plant as a community event. Then it's BYOS- bring your own shovel, and off we go! Just don't let your president stomp on the tree...

"I'm not a tree-huggin' hippy"

Trees don't always need to be planted, sometimes they just a need a hug...of mulch! Most cities and counties have a stockpile of green waste clippings-turned-mulch. Cities spread it everywhere, in parks, on trails, as alternative daily cover on landfills...

• There's usually an abundance of mulch, and, we've found cities and counties will deliver it anywhere if you say you'll do a free "city or county beautification project" with it. Aka, mulching around those sad looking trees and bushes at your company's street border.

• Next, all you need is a bucket and gloves to spread it- I swear! (Bonus points if you get your co-workers Girl Scout troop to help- they are adorable when the bucket is as big as they are). Then, your company will look better, your city will be more cared-for, and your trees will live long and prosper!

"Beach cleanups create as much waste as cleaned up."

Ah, welcome to the world of feeding volunteers offsite. After we first heard this we took a hard look at our annual Beach Cleanup – was it really making a difference, or were we greenwashing? Here's how we sorted it out (pun intended).

• We sorted out alternatives to make cleanups zero-waste. As recycling and composting varies, you start with the end in mind- what can you do in your area? My city does composting in our green waste bins, and has fantastic recycling, so this part was easy for us. We just had to stop bringing anything that doesn't fit into these two categories (grrrr individual chip bags, you ruined our zero-waste event one year!!)

• Add signage and someone stationed at the bins to "guide" people (cute kindergarten classes don't know the difference nor do higher ups at your company), and you're event is now waste neutral before the cleanup even starts.

• For the cleanup, we have reusable kitty litter scoopers and washable reusable bags that groups use to collect the found waste then bring it to the centralized collection point, where it's transferred to a greatly reduced number of bags.

• This is where the fun starts. We have a competition to give a select few prizes to the teams that have the most cigarette butts, the funniest item, the heaviest item, and the most trash.

• This buys us time until the pizza (napkins, greasy cardboard box, and crusts-- all compostable) and sodas arrive (the recycling club mans the bins to get the profits) and the feeding frenzy can begin. Watch out- hungry volunteers are more dangerous than sharks at the beach...

"Networking events are just a waste of time."

You arrive, sign-in, slap on a name badge sticker (that will just stick to your hair in T-minus 30 seconds), then head straight for the bar for a, err, tasty beverage that helps you talk to strangers. Then you try to jump into a lively group's conversation, only to find that they're talking golf, not sustainability. So when they expectantly look to you next, you roll out your only golf joke... What now?

• Now that you've broken the ice, now's the easiest time to segue into something you might be looking for out of the group, like, "I've heard a lot of the local golf courses are changing to recycled water to save costs, too- I wish our company knew how to do that!" You'll get takers that either know something about how to do it (having investigated it themselves), or ones that will take the other route and ask about your company.

• By the end of the networking hour, you've got 10 business cards, and possibly some vendors interested in showing products at your employee eco-fair and a lead about recycled water hookups. If you're interested in a connection with the person/company- don't forget to email them the next working day to say thanks for the chat (and to remind them who you are).

• Oh, and from someone who collects waaaaaay too many business cards, make sure right after the event you write on the back what event you were at when you received it, and any notes (like "Has eco-chocolate contact") that will help you remember who THEY are!

14 COMMUTING

Don't hang your head out of the window when driving...

The world of green cars, commuting, and carpooling can be confusing to everyone. Unless you're just a dog that likes to put your head out of the window with tongue flapping, here are some tips to make your vehicle life at, to, and from work that much D.O.G. gone greener.

"I want to telework, but my bosses think I'll just go to the beach!"

(Whoa- my editing program just underlined the word "telework" and said it didn't recognize those words! Can you imagine that still happening? Bad computer company! Ok, back on topic.)

Did you know the number one group that actually wants to telework is employees at around 10 years into their career (the Gen X's and Y's)? It's not the just-out-of-college set (Millennials, Gen Z)—they are actually worried that if they work from home, they won't have visibility with the boss and won't be able to make it to Vice President by age 25, and they'll miss the comradery of college of dorms and tiny apartments (sounds like a cube already!).

• Those that ARE teleworking are not out at the beach. Those 10 years in (the typical teleworkers) usually have new families, expanding households, and maybe even feel that their boss already knows they are good.

• To encourage employees to discuss this FREE greenhouse gas saving option (after all, you're not driving into work or suckin' power for your laptop!), we put together a free internal Wiki page with Human Resources with info on "Is teleworking right for you?", Technical Requirements, Guidelines, How to approach your Manager, etc.

• By marketing it as a Key Talent Retention strategy, rather than a tree-huggin' hippy plot to overthrow the world, we got approval and the numbers keep growing. Besides-who can read their laptop screen in the glare of the Beach sunshine, anyway?

"I mountain bike all weekend off cliffs! But bike to work - are you crazy?"

Ah, the dichotomy of risk. When it's done for fun, we accept it. When it's even remotely related to work, well, we find excuses. This is what "Bike to Work" week challenges are all for- an excuse to give a prize and pat on the back to anyone willing to put their weekend warrior skills to the test. This is another chance for your eco-network to shamelessly shine.

• Want to reward bikers with breakfast? Get day-old bagels donated by your local grocery store in exchange for promotion of their close location to the office.

• Want to offer an opportunity drawing for prizes or coupons? Have them donated by local bike shops that want your bi-wheeled employees business.

• Then, take pictures of all the bikers in full regalia- helmet, jersey, glasses; even better if it's a group picture (helps hide the helmet hair). Showcase this in your green communications!

• Then, challenge your neighboring companies, and talk some 2-wheeled smack. The more positive visibility you get, the more bike racks you can get from management (seriously, this is almost a 1 to 1 ratio in a competitive environment...).

• Encourage bicycling year-round by allowing bikers free access to the company gym showers.

• You can even find a regulation to help out your case at http://www.bicyclinginfo.org/assistance/. Your company can also help pay for your bike upkeep (www.bikeleague.org) so they can it write off on taxes if using it to bike to work!

"I'd buy a green car, but it's all so complicated"

Arrgggh, it is so hard to be experts in everything! The best research path for our employees? Let someone else do the research and compete for prizes while doing it. This is how we did it.

• We have an annual employee car show at work with a big BBQ from management. We decided to add a green car section, and invited by word of mouth. First year we got a biodiesel, a vanpool van, 6 hybrids, and a Scooter.

• 2nd year, we printed off (on the back of used paper) tear offs that said – "You have a green car! Come show it on XYZ date, and you'll get the best parking spot!" (we just told the organizers our section had to be beside the green team booth as part of our competition, and thus closer in).

• Next year we reached out to the bicycling and other employee clubs, and added motorcycles, recumbent bikes and electric bikes in. The green car section kept growing!

• At our booth, we had trivia, with the answers in BOLD on the green car windshields. Employees fill out the trivia, and get a prize to take back to green their lives (like old company logo drink coasters that we got from surplus office supplies).

• The green car entries got to compete for a green car trophy from the car club.

After getting several years of free research from my employees, I did break down (my car did, too) and bought my new car- a PZEV (partial zero emissions vehicle) 4-door. She (Sharky-yup, I name my cars) was in her first green car show in 2012, and won in 2014!

"I want to get an electric vehicle (EV), but I don't have a charging station at work"

A manager likes to tell the tale of seeing a loooooong extension cord coming out of the back entrance plugged into a EV. He'd gripe, "They can afford a Tesla©! How cheap are they to be stealing power from work?"

For me, I'm glad you want to drive your EV to commute, and I understand your need to charge to get back home. Here's how to help your site fill the EV charger void, too, in a couple of different pathways.

• At first, we tried the usual- do a little research, then asked for some money to put one in at one site. (Hardest way to get money).

• You can broker a better deal with a mass purchase across multiple sites or companies. We found a common unit, created an agreement that gave us leveraged purchasing power, and requested money to go along with the selection.

• You can get "Free" EV charging stations some groups give out to be able to charge your employees an arm and a leg for the ability to charge up.

• We've looked into partnering with a local university's electrical lab. They had a demo unit that a grad student developed for his thesis and we simply allowed the lab access to the data for their research.

Reminder- some of these can take time, but not much effort on a day to day basis can can rev up your EV program (pun intended).

"Our site is HUGE- I can't walk to that building!"

No! That would burn calories- no way am I walking 2 minutes to that meeting! (Wait, I thought we were trying to live a less sedentary lifestyle here?) Ok, here's some solutions we expanded and encouraged to make this "walking" thing less of an issue (in addition to the others like walk routes and bike racks we've already mentioned.)

• Imagine: a big, burly guy going from point A to B as fast as he can on a...tricycle! Not one of those Tonka© Big Wheels, but a real, grown up tricycle with a basket on it for parts, a bell to warn the forklift that he is behind them, and a review mirror to make sure that pedestrian he just whizzed by didn't give him the finger for almost running them over. We have dozens of these tricycles on our site, and the surliest of guys will still ride them, and trick them out for holidays and when their sports teams are winning.

• Late in the afternoon, don't be surprised if you are onsite and you see a janitor with HUGE cases of toilet paper for the upcoming week on a... electric cart. As the sweetheart of rapid onsite transportation (one of our buildings itself is nearly a mile long) these electric carts also get tune ups and carwashes, as their department owners find them invaluable in moving large tour groups, lite boxes, recycling roll offs, and even executives late to meetings, from place to place.

SECTION 6
TALK A GOOD TALK

15 COMMUNICATIONS

Is your Bark better than your Bite?

Wuff! Bark! Growl... what does it all mean? Your communications about and for your sustainability efforts will make or break you. If your D.O.G. isn't making sense, see some of these tips we've used to get our point across. Now, make sure your Bark is better than your Bite!

"Can I give you some (Seeds) of Advice?"

My emails are staging a revolution in my inbox! We're all swamped by email. Here's some eco-tips to help there.

• To streamline the emails our employees were getting our Communications group created a weekly email to employees with all the events upcoming. At the very tip top of that email is a Seeds of Advice column from, you guessed it, the green team!

• The team created a spreadsheet with HUNDREDS of green tips on them (simply google Green tips to find ones for your use from open source sites like EPA and your local utility company), and sent them to our communications group.

• The green team put tips into categories, so if Communications is trying to match a tip up for say, summertime, they can easily find one on water conservation for employee's gardens.

• Just note- if you put metrics in there, and you've got engineers or bored employees in your company, you need to hyperlink to the source, or employees will email you and debate your calculations for how much water you saved with 4 inches of mulch versus plain soil. ("A lot" doesn't always satiate their need to know).

"I've Caught you ~~Red~~ Green Handed"

Hands up! We've caught you red, err, green handed. To be caught in the act of doing something positive and being recognized for it is a very powerful thing.

- We simply ask our employee green members to nominate a peer or team for an exemplary green thing they've seen or heard about being done. The nominations and recognition have run the eco-spectrum:

  - Setting up recycling bins to fundraise for Breast Cancer awareness.

  - Being the first winner of the green car section of the employee car show.

  - Designing a product that needs less hazardous chemicals.

  - Making a Medical form process completely digital.

- The prize is 15 minutes of fame in the company magazine! A short, fun write up, a catchy picture with the employee re-enacting being caught in the act, and an employee's chance to give their own eco-tip at the end of the article and you are done! As the article is on the last magazine page it makes GREEN the final word.

Definition: Articles (Pronounced: Our Tickles)- a piece of writing that communicates information in an interesting and light hearted manner; one that makes you happy you spent the time reading it.

Remember- if something is not fun, why will most employees read it? As you're looking at doing more communications, remember that everyone's time is limited and they want to enjoy what they spend their discretionary time on (thank you for reading this book, by the way! I hope it's been funny/informative for you).

• Green e-newsletter: have someone at the beach cleanup write down the top 10 reasons that the Beach Cleanup rocked (silica sand joke).

• Next, write up those Caught Green Handed mini-articles.

• Graduate to explaining about the green fleet vehicles your supply chain opted for.

• Then submit some positive updates to local green magazines or your local paper about your green car show.

• Then, incorporate it all in your Corporate Sustainability Report (or start one!)

Before you know it, you'll be writing a book about it all (I'm speaking from experience here)!

"Are you on the DL?"

Not the Down Low, the Dis-TRO! (Distribution list) How do you get all your eco-wonderful info out to people? Did you already send that recycling cartoon to Julie and Joe? Did I let the magazine editor know we got another award? As your green team and supporters grow, you'll need to keep track of them.

We make several distribution lists through our email program and other tools to solve our predicament.

• Inside company employee volunteers/supporters. They get the upcoming events lists, small highlights, links to pictures, chances to win small green competitions etc.

• VP and Communications supporters. That includes awards we've recently received, representative pictures at events, short executive blurbs on events for activity reports, and POC's for more information. We've gotten into national news releases for our company this way!

• External supporters. There are retirees, magazines, clubs, authors, government officials, etc that love to know what your company and green team are up to. Add them to this list, but make sure to clear with your Communications team what you submit to it. Outsiders may ALSO turn it news a national story, and it may not be the one you were intending!

Phone/Text

Sometimes word has to spread fast. That's where our phones that we are attached at the hip come in.

• Whether it's a prerecorded greeting or text message that to a list of supporters (that have voluntarily signed up for them), it will be able to call your group to action MUCH faster. As fast you talk or type (yup, I'm talking to you Millennials), these distribution lists can beat you to the draw every time.

16 SOCIAL MEDIA

DOGs like to chase birds.

Use all venues open to inspiring your coworkers! This includes social media (even D.O.G.'s like to chase down eco-news on Twitter...).You'll find which ones your work peers really latch on to, then focus your efforts on those. If your company blocks a specific resource at work, try another! They can't ALL be barking up the wrong tree...

Social Media to Exploit

• **Twitter©**: A Green communication: a birdie telling you Saturday = beach cleanup! Keep <140 characters, and let short-attention-span employees sign up! (that was under the limited 140 characters, by the way!)

• **Wiki© Web Pages**: A team of employees created our own internal Wiki pages, so they could build webpages about programs, awards, highlighting themselves, or teams that they are in without the risk of accidently putting company proprietary information out on the World Wide Web. So we created some wiki pages for our green team (the "programming" is infinitely easier than a real websites). If websites are intimidating to you, try a wiki page. It will take the bite out of virtual communicating!

• **Facebook© page**: Your greenies can sign up, get notified of new calendar items, share links to wonderful green articles, check in at beach cleanups, share pictures of an inspiring peer that's Caught Green Handed, etc. It'll make it easy to get some employee *face* time and get their heads out of a *book* (heheh, that's a terrible pun, indeed!).

• **LinkedIn©** has turned out very useful, as I list our team's awards and accomplishments associated with our team (=lots of views by peers in the industry and requests for us to come speak!).

• **Instant Messaging headers**: Our company provides an instant messenger, and has a header section on our profiles. Instead of rubbing vacation plans in my coworkers faces there (and risking them stealing my office supplies while I'm gone), I use that space to get more volunteers for an event, link to eco-articles, and make dorky mulch-ado-about-nothin' jokes.

17 PAWS OR PRINT

"Paws" before your print.

A former boss liked to tease me when I was hesitant to print out a copy of a presentation. "Ah, the green gal doesn't want to kill a tree!" they'd say. My responses usually included:

- "utilizing existing company resources" (use your laptop computer)
- or "financial affordability of processes" (it costs money to print and buy paper/toner)
- or "worrying about proprietary leakage" (the boss possibly losing the print out).

Did you notice that I didn't say "it's not green"? It's because they don't respond to that. Thus, if you print it, it's gotta be worth it. Hit the "paws" button before you print stuff for your green team and events. Consider some of these that we've done after much trial and error and choose what's best for your team!

"Come Fly(er) away with me…"

I hate printing flyers (even if they are on the back of already used recycling bin materials), though I have found it's hard to beat their use in reaching some employees who don't check their email accounts. Thus, any flyers have to have:

- Impact (graphics and short wording),

- Be appropriately placed so they'll be read (inside of bathroom stalls works very well- a captive audience!),

- A commitment that I go and take them down after the event to recycle (eases my corporate tree-huggin' hippy consciousness).

Freebies

• **Bulletin boards in cafeteria**: We took discarded bulletin and dry-erase boards from the facilities group. These went up in the cafeterias, and we use them to write tips, upcoming events, and show the earth day pledge posters employees signed.

• **Dry erase boards in lobbies**: More discarded dry erase boards! This one gets propped on an old metal book end holder (bend the edge up in the drawer and it becomes an easel!) in the lobby to remind people of an upcoming event. At the end of event- just wipe it, and your eco-consciousness, clean.

• **Posters**: Use the backs of old posters or the back of desktop calendars as the base material for your artistic handiwork and event/program promotion. Or try dry-erase markers on the glossy poster backs- it works just like dry-erase boards! **Remember, if it's a recurring event, make sure it says things like "This Friday" instead of the full date (you can't reuse outdated items easily).**

• **Signs at decision points**: "Lights out" stickers in conference rooms, "battery recycling bin location" info in supply storage closets, ticker with "how many disposable bottles we've avoided" at water fountains. More tech savvy? Post QR code stickers with your green team logo beneath these areas to drive employees to the same info on your green website.

"Can you point me to the recycling?"

Our green team found a couple of ways to communicate where the recycling bins were (because if an employee doesn't know where they are, they are useless!)

- Step 1. Select a common location in all locations- paper beside the printers, bottles/cans near the drink machines/fridge, etc.

- Step 2. A wiki page that shows a map of where they are (and explaining Step #1).

- Step 3. Signs hanging from the ceiling near recycling bins.

Recycling instructions

So, you made up some really cheap/cool paper desktop recycling bins, and you are about to roll them out! Take a moment to do an "intern check" on them.

· Hand the box to an intern and ask "What is this; what do you do with it?" If not intuitive, they won't have a clue. Our intern thought it was an inbox for projects we were giving them. (Um, why wouldn't I have used email?)

· Thus, we created a sticker for the back end of the box that said "Hold white paper recycling here" and a "launch sheet" for the inside that stated:

o We were expanding the paper recycling,
o These are the types of paper we can recycle,
o Here's your own desktop recycler,
o You must empty it into the centralized bin when it is full,
o The centralized recycling bins at the printers.

SECTION 7
WHAT? IT'S NOT ALL ABOUT ME?

18 RECOGNITION & AWARDS

Give a dog a bone...and let 'em be Top Dog.

If you give a D.O.G. a reward, they'll love you 'till the end of time. Even if that bone doesn't have financial value to you or them, there is the sentimentality, the pride in the act of being recognized, and the ability to brag about it! So find some bones to give your D.O.G.'s! They'll overachieve for you every time. Everyone wants to be recognized as the top dog every once in a while

"You can't give an Award to yourself"

Or can you? When your company has competitions for things like safety, quality, affordability or performance, nominate your green team and events! Brainstorm with your group- how did our project X affect Y category?

• For instance: Our Admins without Borders team collects and distributes gently-used surplus office supplies. It saved the company money (affordability), avoided injuries (safety), and increased worker productivity (no delivery wait time), etc. We nominated them in every category that came up that year. They ended up getting also getting high performance ratings from their management from all of the positive press they were getting on the program.

Did they continue doing the supplies collection after that? Absolutely! 15 minutes of fame goes a long way in most company cultures!

"Are we using the USO©?"

Our employees rally around the USO©- it's got locations all over the world, in most of the cities where we had offices, and touches so many people in the USA and abroad, that all our employees probably knew someone in the military that benefitted by this group. Thus, we fundraise for them. Here's our tried and true list for fundraising!

• Green trivia for $1- prizes were giveaways we usually would give to employees to promote sustainability in the company anyway.

• We tried our own nature photo contest- but the pet photo category (dogs in goggles and swim rings) kicked our teams butt.

• Next we did a "Recycling toss" that had the different bins for recycling from around our campus, a stack of recyclables on the table, and you got points for shooting them into the weirdly hanging recycling bins.

• Then we finally hit on the event that is good for the planet, gets swarmed by employees, doesn't cost the company anything but employee volunteers on their lunch break, and takes little preparation. The $1 Reuse Rummage Sale (yup-we're too lazy to make non-recyclable stickers with different prices). Right after the event, our pre-scheduled charity truck comes and takes away the left over materials. It all comes full circle, and there's nothing to store in my tiny cubicle. Yay!

"Who won the e-waste drive competition?"

• A Green Team Travelling Trophy. Simple as it gets. It's a printed PowerPoint© certificate encased in one of those wood plaques with acrylic covering held on by fancy pushpins. I received the plaque for being with company 1 year. (What else would I do with it otherwise?) I pried off the top, printed the new certificate, inserted it, and I reprint and update it yearly.

• When you hand it out- make sure you make a big deal- take pictures with executives shaking the team's hands. Email the pictures to your team, and have the executive display the Travelling Trophy in their awards case. (I use double sided tape and my business card on the back to ensure if ever lost, it gets back to me)

"We changed something in the design and can no longer use these."

WAIT! Your green teams will NOT care- they're into reusing things and not letting them go to waste, right? (and they still like free stuff, no matter how we try to reduce that material side of ourselves) Look for things like these:

• Old company recruiting giveaways- rip out the inset calendar from 2007, recycle the calendar, then give out the goody.

• Random items- stress balls, pens, notebooks, lanyards- left over from employee moves. Even a mish-mash of items is good in a grab bag - not everyone wants the same thing!

• We hope the surfers didn't pee in these...In their wetsuits, that is, while surfing, because we've repurposed the donated/discarded wetsuits to a second life as mouse pads, drink coasters and cozies. Have scissors? That's all you need to make these.

• Did you trash your Desk- Envision huge rolls of materials. These rolls come on a central cardboard tube (like sturdy wrapping paper tubes at Holiday time). Cut the tube down to about 9 inches, cover it in Japanese Washi tape, insert an empty reused water bottle inside of it- TA DA! Acts as a vase for a flower.

"Thank you, Thank you, we ARE Awesome…"

How to find awards to recognize your teams work: search it on the web by simply entering "(your city/county/region here)" and "enviro" and "award" to get a plethora of items back as a start for your award mongering.

• Once you apply for an award, brag about it to others, and like all good businesses and environmentalists, they will try to compete with you.

• Say congrats, and then add their item to your mental registry as your next target for awards applications!

• Keep this going, and you'll end up with an entire display case worth of awards.

• And if you DO WIN, a simple acronym from Dale Carnegie© classes for your acceptance speech that we've used- TOUT- (Thank-Owe-Use-Thank)

• Ex: "Thank you! I owe it to my green team volunteers. We'll use this to further our cause. Thank you again for this recognition."

"It's mine!"

You can always create your own awards-really!

• One year, we won a local non-profit environmental award. Then we joined as members to the non-profit, and showed them how they had a gap in their recognition process for a certain niche area. They created a new category. We won that one, too, 2 years later.

• Coincidence? Actually, yes, because we don't get to be on the awards committee as a conflict of interest). But, creating the visibility of the missing gap (in our case, collaboration with other green teams), we can take credit for!

"Me? Heck, Look at 'We'!"

• To get visibility for the award your team gets, keep giving the awards to your site/office manager in a public meeting and ask them to display them "prominently" (fake British accent works wonders here to impart gravity to the situation).

• If they don't have an awards case they may give you an area to control and display them in! That's how we got an awards case all our very own.

• We filled it up with our green team t-shirts, reusable bags, articles, pictures, and awards. As you get more awards, reduce the other filler fluff and wow people with just how many things you've accomplished.

• I then would make this display case the final stop on any facility tours we did...people really only remember the first and last things you tell them. (What was that previous chapter about?)

19 LEARNING

Teach an old dog new tricks.

I just read the most interesting article that highlighted that the best leaders are the ones who constantly learn-because not only are they well informed, but they're INTERESTING! They have something to talk about around the water cooler. They can branch off of most subjects their teams bring up. Try some of these next areas to keep yourself interesting with new tricks!

"Eww- was that in the bathroom?"

The average prices of the "green" and "leadership" books on my shelf in my office right now (14 last count), run between $18 and $45 (with leadership books costing more than the ones about green business- who says "Green" always costs more?!) Instead of always keeping them to my lonesome self, we create mini sharing libraries. Here are the different ones we've set up at work:

• **Bathroom**: magazines (NOT to read in the bathroom-ladies just tend to swap magazines here before the toilet areas. Men can do the opposite, but please don't pass them to me afterwards!)

• **Break room**: science fiction and any mysteries (my hourly employees love these and read them during lunch and breaks.)

• **Donate to Charity**: Sell them for funds or donate directly to your charity (ask what they like-the USO© really likes recent magazines and books on wars, the women's home really liked children's books for their small kids and self-help).

• **Leadership**: There's a small bookcase in the Directors office- finish your book on the plane coming to the meeting? Donate it here and then borrow a book for the plane ride back to your home office.

• **Business/Topical**: our company has interoffice mail. We have a wiki page that posts what books are available and the POC. Want the book? Drop 'em an email with your office mail stop, and update the wiki page. 2 days later it's yours for the learnin'.

"We never get to learn anything new because we can't pay an instructor."

I'm a whiz at Vermiculture (the raising and production of earthworms and their by-products) and I've got hundreds in a single bin in my garage! (the by-products fertilize my garden).

I'll talk to anyone about worms- kids who visit our house, a past President of our company (he may regret asking about my hobbies), visiting Identity theft experts (we put shredded personal papers and the worms completely destroy it)... and I just taught 50 students how to build their own bin out of coffee cans. Guess how much I got paid? $0. I swear, the look on their faces when taking a handful of worms out for their bins was enough (where they engrossed, or just grossed out?).

So, take a quick poll of your Eco-Chic volunteers to get other free eco-speakers-

• What green skills do they have?

• Do they garden?

• How about making green personal cleaning products?

• Do they drive an eco-car that they love to brag about?

• Don't forget those you invited to your Eco-fair. Since they want new volunteers, participation in a community plan, donations, or to sell employees stuff, they will usually teach a free lunch n' learn (LnL) about their eco-topic.

Those free LnL's are so much cooler than eating my lunch staring at emails at our desks...and they cost the same- $0!

"How will I ever get any of this done?"

• Simple answer? Turn off your email at lunch time. I'm super serious. This is the only way that this book is getting written "write" now (pun intended). I cut the umbilical cord every lunch time when I need to write, meditate, go out to lunch with coworkers, etc.

• I've even gone a step further some days to create "no email" times of the day. My boss calls whenever he needs me urgently anyway, so allowing myself to solely focus on the task at hand makes me more productive.

• And that trend "Oh- we can multitask and do it all at once?" That's bogus. You lose 20% of your brain power while you are trying to "do it all". Think of a computer with too many programs running at once- it slows down, and so would you!

So cut the virtual email cord. Turn it off and get out of there (this works at home with TV's, too, if you're looking to make an impact in your home and community).

20 IN CLOSING

If you're not the lead dog, the view is always the same.

Remember, this will all be a labor of eco-love! Most of these events and ideas took place over the last 10 years of my career. At some point, you'll be like the trees. I'm not sayin' you'll only grow in the summer, bear fruit or that you'll be rigid... but more likely...seasonal. At some point in creating all of this, change will come. Like a tree, don't struggle to hold onto the results of your growth (aka, leaves) – you sometimes need to release things you hold so closely, so you can move forward in your eco-evolution, and prepare for what's next.

You'll come to the point where some of your green efforts are running autonomously, and really don't need to be baby-sat any longer. You'll find with other projects that their usefulness has gone with the sunset and with a new dawn something better will take its place.

You yourself one day may change careers, jobs, or

companies, and thus you'll have to let go of all that you've created there. But remember, as you move onto your next phase, you will have a chance to bud and bloom all over again, and recreate yourself and your projects in your new environment, and those that step in to fill your old shoes can now bloom, too.

Sustainability does not depend on just 1 person- it's a culture change, an awareness that needs to percolate into the very core of a business. It deserves a seat at the decision table, and the only way you'll get to that is by taking the first step yourself, when no one else requires it or is willing to do it themselves. You've inspired others along the way, and can only do so for so long until it needs to stand on its own, for others to be creative out of their own need to be Doing.Our.Greenest. at work.

Now step out on your path to eco-creation, and remember to let those D.O.G.s (Doing. Our. Greenest.) take the lead!.

PS-Still Worried about how to start up a green team and can't get enough of my smart-butt storytelling?

• Listen to my Podcast with Dale Carnegie teacher and Coaching for Leaders Podcast extraordinaire, Dave Stachowiak of West LA College, entitled "How To Get Buy-In For A New Initiative" on #CFLshow http://bit.ly/12lrw8W

• Or follow me on Twitter @Christy_Martens

• Or at my blog at http://BeGreenHeeled.blogspot.com

• Or at http://www.examiner.com/green-living-in-los-angeles/christina-martens

I do frequent tips, from starting up, to keeping up, one green heeled step at a time! Let's, go, D.O.G.!

ABOUT THE AUTHOR

Christina Kull Martens received the 2012 Los Angeles County Chairman's Award for Green Leadership, making her one of the "Greenest People in LA." An environmental engineer by training, she also sits on eco-nonprofit boards, and creates and leads sustainability teams and efforts in Corporate America, while focusing on efficiency, affordability, innovation and project management. She enjoys working with other professionals to solve and prevent environmental problems, and truly believes that working *within* corporations is the next environmental forefront.